Building our Faith Walk

Poems of Faith & Encouragement

Janet Wilson

Janet Wilson

Kingdom Publishers

www.kingdompublishers.co.uk

Building our Faith Walk

ISBN: 978-1-913247-45-4

1st Edition by Kingdom Publishers
Kingdom Publishers
London, UK.

You can purchase copies of this book from any leading bookstore or email
contact@kingdompublishers.co.uk

Dedication

To my husband Robert and church friends who
have encouraged me in my writing.

Contents

Chapter 1
A Poem of Hope

The morning is broken, the night is gone

Bird song fills the air

The sheep are grazing, cattle resting under the bough
of a tree

Children are playing, their voices ringing out

A picture of God's creation for all to see.

The Saviour's guiding hand is here

For all to hold

Heavy hearts will no longer be

Sorrow and sighing will flee away

Songs of joy will come

And the Father's glory will be revealed

With healing in His wings.

Chapter 2
A Song of Praise to God the King.

Sing praises to our God the King

He sits on His throne above

Encircled by His angels adoring Him

Yet He sends down to us His love

Through Jesus Christ His Son.

Come before His throne of grace

Lay your burdens at His feet

Rest in His comforting embrace

Let all worries go

And feel the Spirit's flow.

His living water poured over you

To give you power in this world of woe.

Receive His blessings one by one

Nothing is too hard for Him.

Sing praises to our God the King.

Chapter 3
Call on His Name.

Call on His Name
Call on His name
The Name above all names
The Name of Jesus Christ our Lord.

He is the Saviour of the world
Come to set the captives free
He sat little children on His knee
And said come to Me with a child-like faith
Like these little ones.

He comes to bring hope and comfort
Trust in Him and you will never be alone
No longer tossed about like the waves of the sea
Cherished and loved forever be
Walking in truth and not falsehood
Chosen by the Son of God.

Chapter 4
Easter Day, What a Glorious Day.

Easter Day, what a glorious day
Easter Day, what a glorious day.

When You rose from the dead
And gave us sinners hope
As we put our trust in You
You gave us new life with You.

We begin a new journey following You
Our old life we leave in the past
You take us into pastures new
What glories we find walking with You.

No longing for the old life but embracing the new
Each gift You give us is a blessing from You
Help us live each day living for You.

Easter Day, what a glorious day
Easter Day, what a glorious day.

Chapter 5
Faith not Fear

Walk in faith not fear

Fear cripples us

Faith lifts our spirits

Brings hope not despair

Look to Jesus the Source of light and life.

In these challenging times

Look to Him the Sustainer of all things

He brings healing to the nations

Breathes new life into that which was dead.

His angels watch over us

Singing anthems of praise

To the Glorious One

Who will protect and shield us

Lift us up to worship Him.

Chapter 6
God of all Creation.

God of Creation Who has seen us through all ages

The plagues, earthquakes, floods, and famines

The trials and tribulations of life

All have come to an end.

This current vile virus will also pass

The lockdown will end

Lessons will have been learned

Communities have come together

Compassion increased, may it continue

The beginnings of revival

Until you usher in Your Kingdom

Triumphant King.

Chapter 7
God's Hand in Nature.

Do you hear the buzz of the bee on your plants?

Do you see the butterfly fluttering around?

Do you hear the birds singing in the branches of the lofty trees?

Do you see the tiny ants working hard on the ground?

Do you wonder Whose hand has created the natural world?

Is it our Heavenly Father Who looks down from above?

He commanded life into being.

He will sustain His world as long as He wishes.

Through good and bad times He helps His people.

Trust and obey Him and He will never fail you.

Look to Him for guidance and do not walk in your own strength.

Be joyful and thankful for all His provisions.

Chapter 8
Halleluiah to the King of kings.

God of all faithfulness and truth

We bow the knee and worship You

Joining with the angels' anthem of praise.

Chorus

Halleluiah to the King of kings

Halleluiah to the King of kings

Praise to His name all creatures great and small

Lifting our voices in adoration to the sovereign King

Come and worship Him on high.

Chorus

We bow before His throne of grace

In adoration of the Sovereign Lord

We seek to know His loving ways.

Chorus.

Chapter 9
Hope in the Darkness.

Even in this darkness, where sickness lingers, there are
glimmers of hope

Tales of heroism amongst hospital staff

Stories of neighbours doing good deeds

Helping each other, easing the burden

God's love is all around

Don't leave Him out.

In dark times nature still delights

A babbling brook, fish swimming upstream

A badger in his sett, burrowed from sight

A squirrel leaping from branch to branch in a tree

Insects pollinating plants for all to see

The dawn chorus of birds awakening the morn

The glories of God's creation unfolding.

In these dark days there are signs of hope

Look to the heavens, look to the skies

The saviour is watching over us

One day we shall awaken

To a new and refreshing time.

Chapter 10
In Whom Can We Trust?

When trouble comes, who do we trust?

The Lord of Lords and the King of Kings

He is the One we can trust

He has the whole world in His hands.

Come to Him all ye people

Bow before His throne of grace

He will sustain you, keep you, heal you

There is no one like Him

Believe on His Name, the Name above all other names.

He is our Deliverer, our only Hope

A defender of the weak and helpless

He will bring us out into a spacious place, into new green
pastures

Have faith , not fear

Rise up you saints and take hold of all His promises.

Jesus is the same yesterday, today, and forever.

Chapter 11
Journey of Life

Life is a journey

Not always on a superhighway

Sometimes it takes a lonely road

Which path are you on?

Do you like to be your own boss?

Or do you like someone to follow?

Do you like an easy time?

Or do you enjoy a challenge?

Would you like assurance you are on the right track?

That someone is there watching your back

There is One Who cares and longs for you to go the right
way

Our heavenly Father Who looks down from above.

Chapter 12
Lay Your Burdens at My Feet.

Come all you people, lay your burdens at My feet

And I will do the rest.

When troubles come do not fret or worry

What good does that do?

It does not help to heal the soul

That's what the Lord your God will do.

I come to soothe the troubled brow

And calm the raging storm

So come shelter under My embrace

And feel the warmth of the Good Shepherd's arms

around you.

Chapter 13
Life Changes

In these uncertain times life has changed

Planes grounded, ships not cruising on the high seas

Streets deserted, less traffic on the roads

Shops shut and cafes closed

However less pollution in the air

Parents home schooling, spending more quality time with
their children.

Life still goes on amidst the sadness

The cry of a new born baby is heard

Lambs bleating in the field, calves running to their
mothers

Piglets snorting in their sties

People are helping out each other

Shopping for the elderly and running errands

Enjoying a stroll in the park or a walk by the sea

Taking in simple pleasures

Forgotten in the busyness of life before.

When this pandemic is over

Let us remember the good values practiced in time
of need

Look to the future with intention to follow His lead

To know the Good Shepherd and walk in His ways

Showing His love and compassion to all we meet.

Chapter 14
Our Ever-Present Friend

The majestic eagle flies in the sky
Swooping down to find his prey
The unsuspecting lamb snatched away
In his clinging claws
The African lion hides in the bush
Waiting to pounce on the lone deer
Separated from the rest of the herd.

The Animal Kingdom daily faces friend or foe
Does human kind face the same?
In this current crisis where we are attacking the unseen
virus
Hanging in the air.

There is a Friend Who always stays by our side
The Lord above who guides us on our way
Leads us through the deep dark valleys and on to the
mountain tops
Eventually taking us to His eternal Paradise.

Chapter 15
Rainbows

Rainbows appear when the rain stops and the sun comes
out

A sign of promise made long ago

When the rain stopped over Noah's Ark

God's plan revealed that He would never flood the whole
earth again.

In these times of sickness a rainbow is still a sign of hope

Pictures of rainbows displayed in windows and on doors
along our streets

Children and adults alike painting the vivid colours

Trust in a hope for better times

Awake to a new and happy day.

Chapter 16
Seasons Come and Seasons Go.

Seasons come and seasons go
But the steadfast love of the Lord never ceases
When times are tough and life drags you down
Be still and hear His voice whispering in your ear
I am here with you, always by your side.

He is with you in the calm and storm
On the mountain tops and in the valleys
If you stay on the narrow path
You will not be led astray.

Heed not the mutterings of the world
But listen to the Master's voice
And follow in His footsteps
Show his love and grace to this needy world
Singing His praises everyday.

Chapter 17
Senses.

I see the coming of the glory of the Lord

I hear the sounds of the trumpets heralding His return

I smell the fragrance of Jesus in the air

I taste the sweetness of honey on my lips.

The Bridegroom is preparing His church for His return

Be ready and waiting like the five wise virgins at the door

Do not tarry any longer

For the Lord is coming in all His glory

And His Kingdom will reign for evermore.

Chapter 18
Swim to the Rock of Our Salvation.

Swim to the Rock of our salvation

Swim, swim, swim.

The Captain steers the tiller, He will not let you shipwreck

While you are with Him on the deck

The waves may crash and boulders fall into the sea

But He will guide you safely to shore

Protect you as in the Ark long ago.

You will look back and see His hand

Has led you through the storms

So keep standing on Him

The Rock of our salvation.

Chapter 19
The Breadth of God's Love.

His love is higher than any other

His love is deeper than any other

His love is wider than any other

His love is eternal.

God is with you wherever you go

Flying high in the sky or sailing on the seas

At work or play

In sad and happy times

In sickness and in health.

From the beginning He is with the babe in arms

He is with the single mum in the high rise

Struggling to make ends meet

With the children playing in the backyard

Concerned for the teen grappling to make sense of
the world

The businessman at his desk
The pensioner sitting on a park bench.

Let Him guide you on the right way
And His love will take you through to eternity.

Chapter 20
The Creator's Hand

See the flowers dancing in the breeze

Hear the birds singing in the trees

Look around and see nature in all its splendour

And recognise the Creator's hand at work.

He looks upon the earth

And sees the fragility of man

His heart of compassion is drawn to us

In our suffering He calls out

Words of comfort to encourage

And set us on our way.

Do not dwell on sadness

Look to the Heavens

Be inspired by Him Who made the twinkling stars

Let Him lead you and be refreshed.

Chapter 21
Uncertain Times

In these uncertain times the world is in a time of waiting

Wondering what next action governments will be taking

Are we still going to be in lockdown or unleashed into
some kind of freedom?

It's hard for leaders to take the right action

We need divine intervention.

Let us look to God for inspiration

He can show us the next best move

We long to meet up with our friends and families again

But not too soon lest we spread infection

Let us be wise in His eyes

Then we shall see the way through our troubled times.

Chapter 22
Your Light Shines out of the Darkness

Out of the darkness comes Your light

Out of the rainclouds comes the rainbow

Your covenant agreement with us

Spring is awakening

The flowers are budding, the birds are singing of Your creation.

Do not fear the stormy weather

For My light will break through

Let My Spirit wash away your tears and fears

Let Me light the way in the darkness

Stand firm in the battle which has already been won when I rose on Easter Day.